From a Sinner to a Saint

Danielle Johnson

"We had to celebrate this happy day. For your brother was dead and has come back to life! He was lost, but now he is found!"
Luke 15:32

Dedication

This book is dedicated to the believers and non-believers who are trying to get an understanding of this walk we call salvation. I pray this book is a blessing and a life-changing experience for you as it was for me.

To the believers: As kings of the King, we should desire to become witnesses for our Father. To be witnesses, we must have evidence of the fruits of the Spirit, which is love, joy, peace, patience, kindness, goodness, faithfulness, humility, and self-control (Galatians 5:22). When we show the non-believers that the Father is our provider, that Jesus is the true and living Messiah and that the Holy Spirit is real like we say, that will help them remove that negative stigma and what is portrayed on social media concerning the church. The time has come for us to stop talking and playing church and start showing the world that we serve a true and living God. Our lives should be a testimony to everyone that the Word of the Father is life and love. If we want a life of abundance, we must continually speak, think, and live positive lives. Our goal is to add souls to the Kingdom.

To the non-believers: I pray that this book will be life-changing for you as it was for me. I pray that Jesus will give you the courage to take that step and give your life to the one who created you, the Father. When I decided to give my heart to the only one that matters, Jesus Christ, it was a decision I had to make all by myself. I lost a lot of friends in the process but gained a whole new life. Living your life for God could be lonely at times, and there are some who may not understand your walk. People will leave you, but know that the Father's Word says, *"So, be strong and courageous! Do not be afraid and do not panic before them. For the Lord your God will personally go ahead of you. He will neither fail you nor abandon you."* (*Deuteronomy 31:6*)

Some people have even told you that you will never amount to anything, but the Father says, *"For I can do everything through Christ, who gives me strength."* (*Philippians 4:13*)
You have tried everything, and everybody has failed you; now it's time to try Jesus. Remember, no matter what you lose, there's nothing like gaining the Father, Son, and Holy Spirit.

Acknowledgments

First and foremost, I would like to give glory and honor to the Creator of all things my heavenly Father, for blessing me with the gift of writing. I count it a privilege and honor to be used in this way. If it weren't for His grace and mercy that followed me all the days of my life, I wouldn't be here today. He kept me in my right mind when things should have made me crazy; He loves me even when I do not love myself; He is faithful even when I am not faithful. He loves me despite of me. Lord, you are everything to me, you are the rock that I stand.

I can't go on without acknowledging the most wonderful person that has come into my life and made me the woman that I am today, my son Zion. You are the apple of my eye; I thank the Lord for blessing me with an amazing son. You are very intelligent, smart, funny and the joy of my life. I could not have asked for a greater son; I love you very much. Zion, you are my inspiration and the reason why I strive for greatness and a better way of life. My prayer for you is that the Father will keep you safe; that He will prosper you and keep you in perfect health. My desire for your life is that you will grow into the king He created you to be. And with the guidance of the Holy Spirit, it will be so.

To my church family and friends, old and new; the seeds that has and are being planted in me has blessed me and continues to push me forward. It makes me challenge myself to be a better servant to the Father. I know the Father has greater things for you individually and as a ministry. Get ready for the blessings that you wouldn't have room enough to receive. I pray that the Father will continue to cover all of you with His favor.

I want to thank my family for everything. You have been amazing. Thank you for always being there for Zion and me. No matter what, you guys have never stopped supporting me; for that, I am grateful. I love you all. May the Lord bless you and cover you in His favor.

To my BFF (lol) Theresa Harrison, thank you for always being there for me. No matter what I need, you are always there. The humble heart that you have is going to open so many doors for you. I have learned throughout our friendship when you find a true friend, never let anything come between the two of you. I am grateful that I can call you friend. I shine, you shine, we shine together! Get ready for that tsunami blessing that the Lord is about to bestow upon you. It's well deserved. I love you forever!

*"For God speaks again and again, though people do not recognize it.
He speaks in dreams, in visions of the night, when deep sleep falls on
people as they lie in their beds."*
Job 33:14-15

Dear Readers,

I would like to state that this book is not to dehumanize anyone as a person. The choices that you make are yours and yours alone. My sole purpose of writing this book is to show you that no matter what you have done; the Father can still use you for His purpose. My desire is that everyone who encounters this book will see themselves on every page. I pray that you will allow the Father to show you that His grace, mercy, and forgiveness is real. The choices that I made did not glorify His name nor did it please Him in any way, and that is why I had to make a change. Please know that this book is about me and me alone and my journey to deliverance.

Shalom

Prologue

In October 2005, the Father spoke to me in a dream and said that He wanted me to write a book. He gave me the title and told me how it would change lives. When He first told me to do this, I thought about my past. Instead of being obedient to the vision He had given me, I went to people asking them if I should write about my hurtful experiences. I was told by several people not to put everything I have gone through in this book. I later realized when it's His will, it must be done His way, no questions asked.

The Father said that this book will change lives. My question to everyone was, "How can I help change lives if I didn't tell people about my life?" Sometimes people need to hear from someone who has experienced similar or the same things they have. Christians should be relatable, understanding, and compassionate if we want to reach lost souls.

We must be as transparent as we can, instead of pretending to be so Holy, acting as if we always maintain the image of God. I want to give readers an outline of my life. If you are to experience His Glory, then you need to understand my story. Some may not agree with what I've written, and that's ok because this wasn't written for everyone to agree with me, it was written so people will know that there is someone out here that is or has experienced what they are going through.

So, from my heart, I asked that you pray to the Lord to open your hearts, minds, and eyes. I am about to take you on a journey into my world, a journey that brought me "From a Sinner to a Saint."

"I love you, Lord; you are my strength. The Lord is my rock, my fortress, and my savior; my God is my rock, in whom I find protection. He is my shield, the power that saves me, and my place of safety. I called on the Lord, who is worthy of praise, and he saved me from my enemies."

Psalm 18:1-3

Chapter One

I was born on February 11, 1974, to Eugene and Pearl Johnson. My mother was 34, and my father was 39 years old when they gave birth to me. I am the youngest of nine children: four girls, and five boys. Growing up, I was jealous of my sisters and brothers because they had the opportunity to spend a lot more time with our parents than I did.

My father died when I was one year of age. Being that young, I didn't remember a lot of things about him. When I asked my brothers and sisters about the kind of man that my father was, they would always speak very highly of him. They told me that he liked to watch wrestling and that he used to put me in front of the television to watch it with him. I guess that's why I grew up loving wrestling, and at one point, so did my son. We lived in a big house in the middle of a cemetery. Thank goodness I was a baby then because if I were older, I would have begged my parents to move, and if that didn't work; I would have moved in with relatives. My brothers and sisters told me that the house was fun and scary at the same time. They used to run to the house without stopping because they were so scared to walk through the cemetery. I asked one of my sisters why in the world were we living in that house. She told me that our father was loved by so many people that someone blessed him with it. Ok, I understand that and believe me, I never question any kind of blessing, but I really think I would've thought that one through! There's no way I could have lived in the middle of a cemetery... nope, not happening, I'm just saying.

They also told me how stern he was; there were times when he was at work, and they would run around the house having a good time; they would hear his truck pull up and run quickly to their seats. He wasn't an abusive man; it's just that his presence spoke authority. In my family, my father was the disciplinarian. With having five boys, that was the best decision my mother could have made, like the Bible states in ***Proverbs 13:24, "Those who spare the rod of discipline hate their children. Those who love their children care enough to discipline them."*** From what my brothers and sisters have told me he held onto those words because no rods, sticks or switches were spared on those behinds. My father would tell my mother that she needed to help with the disciplining of the children because he wouldn't be there forever and not soon after, my father died at the age of forty. In an instant, she became the father as well as the mother.

My father had very limited education, he stopped going to school in the sixth grade, but he always found a way to provide for his family. I often wished that my father was still living, maybe I would not have experienced some of the things I did growing up. I believe there comes a point in a girl's life when she needs her father. And Lord knows I needed him. We tend to think that a father is important to a boy, but a girl needs her father as well. A father truly plays a huge part in his daughter's life. She needs a place to run when she does not feel safe in the world. She needs to be shown how a man is supposed to treat her and how she is supposed to treat a man. She needs to hear how beautiful and loved she is, so when those knucklehead little boys try to whisper those words in her ear, she will be able to say with confidence, "I know, my dad tells me that all the time."

When my father died, my mother often worried a lot because everything fell into her hands. I cannot imagine the kind of pressure she was under; like my dad she had limited education, she didn't have any job skills, and she was a widow with nine children. My mother leaned and depended on Jesus. And with all that was going on in her life, I now understand why. She loved Jesus, and she never stopped seeking Him; she never stopped praising Him, and most importantly, she never stopped trusting in Him. She would take me to church with her, and I would fall asleep in her lap while her favorite song "Amazing Grace" was being sung. After a few years, she started to get used to being a widow and a single mother. At least that is what I thought. I mean, here was a woman who lost her husband and was left with nine children to raise all by herself. Never once did she look stressed or defeated. She wore God's peace very well.

I know my mom probably did everything she could to keep us in the house we grew up in, but it became too much for her to maintain. We eventually had to move to the projects.

That move was a culture shock for me, a different environment, and new faces. I guess, fearing the outside drew me closer to my mother inside, but unknowingly to me, it would be the inside that would scar me for the rest of my life. That house in the projects is where all my hell began.

I was about four or five years old when a close family relative called me into his bedroom. What happened next was something I will never forget. He told me to pull down my panties and lay down on the bed. Being a little girl who trusted him, I did what he said. Still not knowing what was going on, I didn't put up much of a fight when he got on top of me, then he proceeded to put himself in a place on me that should never have been touched by anyone! I can remember so vividly the noise he made and the wet stuff on my legs. He told me not to tell anyone, and out of fear, I did not. I never understood why he would do something like that to me, why would he want to hurt me.

After the molestation, I began to develop habits that puzzled my mother.

The first time she became suspicious was one day when we were sitting in the living room, she was on the phone talking to another family member, and I began to rub myself against things. My mother could not understand what I was doing and why it was happening, so she asked a relative to come and talk to me to find out what was wrong. Needless to say, no one ever asked the right questions, and I never told.

My life went downhill after that. I attended this elementary school as a little girl, it was a nightmare. I would get bullied a lot, there were times I would run home and drop to my knees as soon as I would get home. My mom would bake cookies for me to help me feel better. The cookies worked well, at least until they were gone, and then I would think, "tomorrow it starts all over again." Anyway, my mother was there to make it all better.

Consequently, soon after that, my mother started getting very sick. All the worries brought on stress, the stress brought sickness, and she never got better. I lost my mother at the age of six to a brain aneurysm.

I remember that day as if it were yesterday. I was upstairs when I heard a loud scream; I got up and went downstairs, as I got to the bottom of the steps my brother came running out of the living room. He went into the kitchen, and I heard the silverware being moved around. As he was doing that, I peeked around the corner to see what was going on.

I noticed my mother standing up, looking like an angel. She had on a long white gown, her hair was pulled back in a ponytail, her arms were stretched out, and she had her head back looking up to the sky. As I stood there looking at her, my brother came back into the room with a spoon in his hand. Somehow my mother ended up on the floor; my brother took the spoon and put it in her mouth.

I do not remember how I got to the hospital or who called the rest of the family, but everyone was there. My brothers and sisters went into the room to see my mother. As the door was closing, I started crying for my mother, the last thing I saw of her was her feet, that pain is still surreal. I just kept thinking if she could hear my voice calling out to her, she would have fought harder to stay alive. The way I saw it, a mother would do anything for her child. An ex-girlfriend of one of my brothers would not allow me to go in with them. She kept telling me that I was too young to go inside the room.

I held anger for a long time towards her because I kept thinking that if she would have let me go in to see my mother, then she would have never died. It was twenty years later before I finally talked about this with her. She explained to me why she didn't let me see my mother. Because I was so young, she felt like I would not have been able to handle it, so she tried to protect me. I understood what she was saying but back then all I wanted was my mother.

I also held anger towards the relative who molested me when I was a little girl. I eventually gathered enough nerve to ask him why he did that to me. He said he couldn't explain why but he made sure to let me know that his wife and church didn't know anything about his past. I guess that was a hint for me not to say anything about it. If only he knew how much damage he caused me mentally, physically and emotionally. Because of what he did, no one was worthy of my trust. I felt like I was no good to anyone.

There came a point in my life that I knew it was time for me to heal. To do that, I had to forgive my brother's ex-girlfriend and the relative who sexually abused me. It was the only way I would be able to move on with my life. To be honest, at the time I was thinking: after all that hurt, pain and hell they took me through...despite all of that, I must forgive these people? I heard the voice of the Lord say, "Yes, and here's why, if you want Me to forgive you and not only hear your prayers but answer them, then you must do the same." *Matthew 6:14-15 says, "If you forgive those who sin against you, your heavenly Father will forgive you. But if you refuse to forgive others, your Father will not forgive your sins."* Even though this scripture was a hard one for me, it was something I had to do, I mean it's in the Word, and that settles it.

I had to realize that no matter how much he hurt me as a child and even though my heart was heavy from the loss of my mother, I had to forgive. If I wanted to be set free from the bondage of anger, hurt, and the pain I carried, I had to release those individuals that caused me that pain. Trust me, it was a difficult and uncomfortable thing to do. However, despite how I felt, it had to be done.

"Listen to my prayer, O God. Do not ignore my cry for help! Give your burdens to the Lord, and he will take care of you. He will not permit the godly to slip and fall."

Psalm 55:1 & 22

Chapter Two

After the death of our mother, my siblings sheltered me a lot. I never got the chance to mourn her. I guess they thought it would be best to keep me sheltered so I would not fill the pain of losing her., but I felt it nonetheless. One of my sisters had three children of her own, but she was still willing to seek custody of me. I spent a lot of time at her house, I guess that's why I feel more like a sister to her children rather than their aunt. We had some great times together. However, I can't fully remember my life from the age of six to twelve years old. Even while writing this book, I still couldn't recall those six years.

My sister told me that I had birthday parties, but for some reason, I don't remember any of them. It's like I went to sleep at the age of six and woke up twelve. I often wonder and ask myself several questions seeking answers about those missing years. What happened to those six years? What event took place that made me block out six years of my life? Could it have been the stress of losing my parents or being molested and not being able to tell anyone? Why was I the one they decided to molest? What was it about me? So many questions were running through my mind. At the time, all I could say was, "Lord, give me clarity!"

At the age of thirteen, the same relative who molested me when I was a little girl tried it again, can you believe that. I was babysitting for one of my sisters, and he came over to the house. I was still terrified of him (even to this day) because of what he did to me when I was a little girl. I just sat there pretending to watch television when he asked me if I wanted to "do something" with him. I couldn't believe it; he said it as if it was a normal question or something that someone asks their family member every day. I don't know where the courage came from, but I looked him in his face and told him no! Just like that, with no remorse or emotion, he said ok and left the house, that was the last time he ever approached me like that again. Even though the abuse with him stopped, there was still much more to come. I was molested again by several other men; although they didn't penetrate me, all the unwanted touching was just as bad and damaging to me as a person.

I remember an unpleasant encounter with someone who was close to my brothers. I can't remember how old I was at the time, but he came into my room and proceeded to remove my bed covers and touch me in places that were very uncomfortable. I laid there pretending like I was asleep hoping he would stop, but he didn't. My cousin, who was in bed at the time, stirred and that startled him, he left my room, and I don't think I've ever saw him again after that night.

Another encounter I experienced was with a family member's boyfriend, he too would come into my room. I would wake up to him standing there smoking a cigarette, drinking a beer just watching me sleep; of course, the bed covers would be removed from me. He would then leave out of the room and the next day act like nothing happen. One morning when he was leaving for work, he was watching me sleep again, but this time he touched me on the butt. I told the family member what was going on and I could never under-stand why he was still there. I used to think that if it was one of their children, he was doing that too; the outcome would have been different. I always thought they never believed me. But I later found out that they would sit up and try to catch him, funny isn't it, you would've thought my Word was enough. I guess they dealt with it the only way they knew how. Once again, I asked myself, "why me?"

"Don't be afraid, for I am with you. Don't be discouraged, for I am your God. I will strengthen you and help you. I will hold you up with my victorious right hand."

Isaiah 41:10

Chapter Three

By the time I became a teenager, my self-esteem was so low, I would do anything to fit in with everybody else. I began smoking marijuana and drinking at the age of fourteen. I would smoke from the time I woke up until the time I went to bed. So, you can imagine how my grades were in school; whenever I went, I eventually dropped out in the ninth grade and never looked back. My friends and I started a gang called The Female Temper Crew. We would steal, spray paint buildings, and always fight, sometimes for no reason at all. We would do anything to get into trouble.

For instance, my cousin and the girl next door used to date this guy. Every day they would pick on us and what made matters worse is that we all attended the same middle school; the harassment never stopped. One day as we were exiting the school bus, one of the sisters pushed me, and the fight began.

During this time, my nephew and his friends had their little gang started called Paradise Posse, and they were fighting as well. It was like a riot broke out. While we were fighting, the assistant principal came over to break up the fight, I didn't see her, so I swung and hit her in the face. There was no talking my way out of that; of course, she immediately gave me a ten-day suspension.

As a teenager, I fought a lot, and sometimes the individuals were friends. I remember one fight, my cousin, who was pregnant at the time, walked up to me crying because her boyfriend was cheating on her with one of our friends. As we listened to her, the girl she was talking about walked up to us. Before I knew it, my cousin hits her, the rest of us jumped in and beat her up. We beat her out of her clothes; she ran home naked. I know it doesn't sound right, but it was a cool thing to do at that time. I didn't care how that made the girl feel. Even though I wasn't behaving like a friend, my thought was, "I finally had friends, and that was enough." But what I didn't know at the time is that I was living a life of destruction. My life was heading nowhere fast, and I was taking people with me.

As time went on, I became wilder. I didn't care about anything or anybody but myself. I believe the sexual abuse I encountered early in my life made me not value myself as a young lady. Because of my low self-esteem, I never thought I was pretty enough or worthy of anyone's love. So, to fill that void, I started using my body as a tool to get the attention that I was so severely seeking. Even though I was molested at an early age, I still considered myself a virgin. The first time I had actual consensual sex was when I lost my virginity at the age of fifteen, and it was nowhere near what I expected it to be. I thought my first time would be with someone who truly loved me and treated me with respect. But the guy I decided to be with didn't meet any of my expectations. He took me inside of a vacant house where we had sex, and just like that, it was over.

I felt horrible after it happened, but I kept giving myself to him. I guess I was using sex to get love while he was using love to get sex. I had gotten to a point where it didn't matter how a guy treated me. If I was getting attention from him, it was okay. Sadly, thinking like that lead to bad decisions.

When I was about sixteen years old, two of my girlfriends and I met these guys; we talked to them for a little while before they asked us to ride with them. As we are riding around, one of the guys suggests that we go back to his place. When we got there, we sat around watching movies and pigging out. Eventually, it started to get late, one of us stated that we were ready to leave. They told us that we had to sleep with them for them to take us home; we thought it was a joke at first until we realized they were serious. Because we were so young and didn't know where we were or what to do, we slept with them. Those were the type of situations I continued to put myself into and thankfully none of them cost me my life. I wasn't careful about anything that I was doing or who I was around while doing these things. When I think about how reckless I was behaving and the danger I put myself in, all I can say is, "my goodness... thank you, Jesus."

Another incident took place when a relative was having a party for her husband. She invited the family over. As the night went on, my cousin's boyfriend saw me and asked if I wanted to smoke marijuana with him. I said yes and proceeded to light the blunt; I didn't know that some guys were watching us during this time. When we finished smoking, he went back to the party. The guys approached me and asked if I wanted to smoke with them as well. I started smoking with them, and immediately I started feeling strange; it was like I was floating. Although I could feel them touching all over me, I couldn't fight them off. It was like I was having an out of body experience. I could see and feel what they were doing to me, but I couldn't do anything to stop them. After a while, they took me by the arm and told me to walk to their car with them. Not being able to say no, I went along.

As they led me towards the fence that led to the parked cars, I felt a tug on my arm; it was my cousin. She asked them what they were doing, and they commented: "We are going for a walk." In turn, she said, "go ahead, but she is not going," of course they became upset and started saying mean things, but she didn't care. Eventually, they walked away. I thank my Father continually for His protection because if it wasn't for Him sending her to get me, I could have been raped or killed. I told you this story is real, and I'm letting it all out, no holds bar and no shame. I genuinely believe that someone out there is being careless with their life and is in dire need of someone to come along and move them out of their destructive pathway. I thank God that He has chosen me to be that person by sharing my life story.

Now don't get me wrong, this was a harrowing story to tell because I had to relive some hurtful things that I would rather forget. However, it is my life. It is my truth.

"Thank you for making me so wonderfully complex! Your workmanship is marvelous—how well I know it."

Psalm 139

Chapter Four

If you do not know your self-worth, you become vulnerable and run into individuals who will take what little self-worth you have left. I never thought I would ever be in a relationship with someone who not only abused drugs but abused me as well. No one ever told me the kind of person he was until I was deep into the relationship. If I spoke up for myself, he would fight me simply because someone told him to do so or if I wouldn't give him any money, which was why he would fight me in most cases.

Yet, I stayed. At the time, I thought I was in love and that he would stop being abusive, but he didn't. He hit me once more, and that was the straw that broke the camel's back. I pressed charges against him and that became my way out. He was arrested a few weeks later, and he hasn't been a part of my life since. His friends were upset with me, but I didn't care. I had to do what was best for me to save my life. I believe that if it weren't for me pressing charges, I probably would have stayed in that abusive relationship for a long time.

A few years later, I saw him, and he apologized to me for all that he had done. I forgave him, not to release him but to free myself. I couldn't hold onto any anger or bitterness towards him. Honestly, it would not have done me any good. And now that I know my worth, I will NEVER again settle for less. However, the story doesn't end there. When your self-esteem is so low, you will deal with or do just about anything to feel loved or accepted.

In playing the enemy's games and allowing him to have complete control over me and the decisions I made, he started to bring more demonic spirits into my life.

I began growing appetites for things that I thought at the time were exciting and acceptable. I was falling into desires that were destructive to my Spirit. I realized that the devil could also give you the desires of your mind, especially if those desires are made known to the enemy. The feeling of being with other women became so strong that I could not fight the temptation any longer; I had to be with a woman.

I began having encounters with several women, including close friends. It seemed as if no one was off-limits. And even though it made the friendship change and, in most cases, end, I didn't care not one bit. No matter how terrible and disgusting I felt, it was as if I couldn't stop. I didn't know what to do; all I knew was that I was enjoying it. The first encounter I had was with a dear friend, and even though it was a mutual thing, the relationship suffered tremendously. We are no longer friends and that hurts the most, but like I stated, at that time, I didn't care about anything. Now, please understand even though I was doing sinful things, there were times that I would seek out God for answers, but I don't think I was searching as hard as I was lusting after what I desired. My heart wasn't sincere at all, not like it should've been. Paul affirms in **Philippians 1:10,** *"For I want you to understand really what matters, so that you may live pure and blameless lives until the day of Christ's return"* In the Amplified Bible it says, *"with hearts that are sincere you may not stumble or cause others to stumble."*

This hit home for me. But, at the time of my disobedience, I didn't know that my actions were not only causing me to stumble but others as well. It never was a thought of what I was doing to other people. I was very selfish, and if I kept indulging in that sinful act, I would eventually fall, and so would others. But as I said, I did not care!

As time went on, I hated the way I was living more and more. I wanted to stop everything; smoking, having sex with men and women, and all the things in my life that were not pleasing to God. Have you ever been tired of something? I mean tired, to the point that you were tired of being sick and tired? Well, that was how I was feeling, and even though my flesh was being **satisfied**, my heart was still **dissatisfied**.

My spirit was crying out for a change because there was no happiness, love, joy, and most of all, no peace when I was living that life. I thought it was fun and exciting, but what it was doing was tearing me apart mentally, physically, emotionally, and spiritually. I realized that having sex with someone of the same sex or someone you are not married to; isn't about love. It is about fulfilling the lust of the flesh. It's only a lustful desire that is not of the Father. God's desire is for one man to marry one woman and be fruitful. ***Genesis 1:27-28*** *says, "So God created human beings in his own image. In the image of God, he created them; male and female he created them. Then God blessed them and said, "Be fruitful and multiply. Fill the earth and govern it".* God said that He created us in His image. His desire was for mankind to populate the earth. He spoke into the Spirit of man and said, **"be fruitful and multiply."**

The more I drew to the lifestyle of fornication and homosexuality, the more I was being pulled away from God. I felt His presence slowly leaving me. I felt like I was uncovered, naked, and outside in public for the world to see. It seemed like when people looked at me; they could see the sins I was committing. At that time, I believed that my sins outweighed the wrongdoing of everybody else's sins. When God says that we are not to do something and do it anyway, we are walking in sin, no matter the offense. When I was with someone of the same sex, smoking, and drinking, and amongst other things, I was dishonoring and disrespecting Him. To God, same sex is an abomination unto Him. When we practice homosexuality, it is a detestable sin **(Leviticus 18:22)**. Also, to God, being sexually active with anyone other than your spouse is a sin. He tells us that we must run from sexual immorality because no other sin affects the body as this one does **(1 Corinthians 6:18).** He also says that He will destroy anyone who destroys their temple because your temple is holy and should remain pure **(1 Corinthians 3:17).**

As you can see, no matter the offense, God will still look at it as sinful. In a nutshell, I was living in total SIN! Problem was, I did not realize that I was taking so many other souls with me. Once He showed me what I was doing, it broke me down; spiritually, I was a total wreck. I didn't know where to turn or whom to confide into about my darkest secrets. One of my biggest challenges is worrying about what people say or think about me. Even though I'm close to certain people and knew they wouldn't judge me, I still thought, "how can I go to them and tell them something like this." Like everything else, I bottled it up and never spoke about it. No one knew the lifestyle I was living nor; did they know how I was feeling and because of that the enemy used my vulnerability to his advantage by easing his way into my life once again.

I began to confide in a married friend about everything I was going through. The more we hung out and talked, the closer we became. The truth is the guy was giving me that attention that I craved so bad. And eventually, we ended up in a relationship.

I knew it was wrong, but it was that attention he gave me. It was like a drug that drew me to something that I knew could hurt or destroy his family. But, as I said, I did not care about anything or anybody. He would buy me things and say all the right words a girl wanted to hear. When a young girl or woman hears compliments that make her smile and has not slept with that person, it can leave a sister in a very vulnerable state.

I stayed in that unhealthy "relationship" for five years. Nothing came from it but heartache, pain, and a pregnancy which resulted in an abortion. Shocked that I said that tad bit information? I told you this testimony is raw and real. And finally, sis ain't shamed to tell her full story.

My life was a mess. Through all of this, I was dying inside, and the Lord was slowly removing Himself away from me. I did not know which way I was going; right or left, up or down, front or backward; my emotions were all over the place. I had reached a point where I could not take any more hits to my spirit man. I had to make a choice that would lead to change.

We all have choices, and God has given us free will. It is up to us which paths we will follow. Your deliverance will be based on the choices you make and what you do moving forward. Yes, God is a deliverer, but you also have a part to play in your deliverance. Change starts with you. I was getting tired and if you are tired of the way you are living, then change the way you think. Once again, this is my life story, and I'm going to keep it one hundred!

"I planted the seed in your hearts, and Apollos watered it, but it was God who made it grow. It's not important who does the planting, or who does the watering. What's important is that God makes the seed grow."

1 Corinthians 3:6-7

Chapter Five

The foundation was there, my mother planted that seed years ago, so I had no choice but to walk towards what was familiar. Proverbs 22:6 *says, "Direct your children onto the right path, and when they are older, they will not leave it."* The day that I decided to live my life for Christ was the best decision I have ever made. I started to see how things in my life should be. I begin to see myself as God saw me, as the woman He created me to be. I separated myself from everything that I was use too and began to spend more time with God. Even now I find that I must separate myself because there are times, I can get so caught up in the ways of the world that I would sit God on the mantel. During this time, the enemy will distract you with foolish things that will throw you off the course that God has laid out for you. Need an example, continue reading.

I received Jesus as my Savior in 2002, and I was still living my life like a sinner. I was spiraling out of control. There was no limit to the things I did. I was doing things that were so displeasing to God. I knew the choices I was making were the reason why my life was full of destruction, darkness, despair, pain, un-forgiveness, hatred, and deceit. I felt so ugly inside. Any negative word that goes against what the Lord says about us is how I was feeling.

I heard a wise woman once say, "fulfilling your flesh is like smacking God in the face". That was my light bulb moment. When the light bulb finally came on, the desire to want more began to burn deep within me. I said to myself, "ok, Danielle, now is the time." At that very moment, I was ready to take my walk with God, not just a step further, but take it seriously. Can you think back to the time of your salvation, the season when the Father called you out of that dark, meaningless life and into His arms of salvation? What about your time of healing, prosperity, and deliverance? These times of redemption are according to your season. When you look at your life, you can see how He did everything in His time, His way, but in YOUR season. Once I knew what season I was in, I took hold of it and understood why I was going through the hell I was going through and, most importantly, where I was in my spiritual walk.

Discerning Your Six Spiritual Seasons will provide you with the same wisdom and knowledge that got me through those trying times. There are seasons in our lives that the Father wants us to understand in order to defeat the enemy and destroy the strongholds in our lives.

In this chapter, I will discuss those six seasons in detail so you will be able to determine where you are and how to receive your blessings. If you apply them to your life, they will change you and help bring everything you do not understand into perspective.

Season 1: Developing Your Heart

To receive the Word of God, you must first prepare the ground of your heart, Jeremiah 17:9-10 states; *"The human heart is the most deceitful of all things, and desperately wicked. Who really knows how bad it is? But I, the Lord, search all hearts and examine secret motives. I give all people their due rewards, according to what their actions deserve."*

Being that we cannot trust our own heart, we must leave it all to the Lord who knows our hearts' nature and judges every man fairly.

Those who have a redeemed heart are the only ones who can live in a proper fellowship with the Lord. If we want a changed life, we must first remove things from our hearts that hinder God from entering our lives. Sometimes we get so caught up in our daily lives that we make God last. The Lord should be the only person sitting on the throne of our hearts. Yes, it is ok to love your spouse, children, job, or whatever else that is important, but the Lord should always come first.

In our walk with the Lord, we must see things as He sees them. To Him, it is not what goes in us, but what comes out. In Mark 7:21-23, Jesus tells His disciple that from a person's heart come evil thoughts, sexual immorality, theft, murder. The chapter goes on to say, thoughts of *"adultery, greed, wickedness, deceit, lustful desires, envy, slander, pride, and foolishness. All these vile things come from within; they are what defile you."*

After reading these two verses, now can you see how crucial it is that we make sure that our hearts are pure? If it's filled with evil, then evil is what will come out, but if you fill it with good things, then good things are what you will release.

When I decided to get saved, preparing my heart was one of the most important things I had to do. The steps I took to do this was to make sure I attended a weekly bible study, Sunday services, pray, read his word, meditated on the word, and apply what I learned to my life. When you are taught the Word and choose not to act on it, you cannot experience the blessings attached to being obedient.

Season 2: Inserting the Seed

There are many ways that we can sow, and we all know that money is one of those ways. However, sowing can be through giving your time by serving others, or it can be through speaking a kind word into someone's spirit. God will provide you with more seeds to sow when you sow what you have. Throughout my walk with Christ, I would not allow my circumstances to rule over me. I had to make sure that whatever I sowed would reap a harvest and what I planted was inserted into good soil. When we nurture God's Word, we are letting Him know that we not only care for his Word but that we also cherish it. Our desire is for His Word to become active in our lives. It is one thing to hear something that can help you, but it is different when you apply what you heard, and it changes your life.

So, I ask, how can you expect a change when you do not apply what you have learned, make efforts to change, or share what you learned by planting into others' lives? When we follow the Kingdom principle of Matthew 6:33, we will be blessed. It is just that simple. You are only fooling yourself if you think otherwise. *"But don't just listen to God's word. You must do what it says. Otherwise, you are fooling yourselves"*. (James 1:22).

Season 3: Scattering the Seeds

The process of fertilizing a substance is to increase growth. Once you have received the Word, you must guard your heart and that Word. During this season, the enemy will throw anything at you to make you lose focus. He will use strangers, friends, your spouse, and even family members to get under your skin. The enemy's goal is to make you lose the Word that you received in your Spirit. He wants to take the one thing that gives you power, and that is the Word of God.

Let us look at this through the eyes of a farmer. When a farmer fertilizes the soil, his objective is to make sure that the planted seeds will grow. To do this, he must toil the ground and nurture it. When it comes to the Word of God, we should be the same way. The enemy will try to cloud your mind with so many negative things to make you doubt God's Word. His sole purpose is to blind your mind. The powers of evil are helpless to do anything unless they first have gained ground to man's will, emotions and body.

If you allow the enemy to take control of your mind, he has you. He can work freely without asking for an invitation.

After I got out of the relationship with the married guy, I remember being in prayer one night and the enemy saying to me, "He does not hear you. Look what you did. I don't know why you are on your knees. You might as well get up." And just like that, I would stop praying. See, the enemy planted negative thoughts in my mind. The enemy's goal is to distract you and keep you from being in fellowship with God. He wanted me to believe that God no longer loved me. He wanted me to think that my sin was not forgiven. But God said in Romans 8:1, *"So now there is no condemnation for those who belong to Christ Jesus."* So, when those thoughts of doubt, fear, worry or self-loathe come; your job is to cast down those imaginations (2 Corinthians 10:5).

In Cindy Trimm's book, Commanding Your Morning Daily Devotional, she said that he gave His disciples not only an outline of what to pray for daily but also a starting place for consistently knocking on the door of heaven. She says that transforming their minds from a world of doubt, oppression, and failure into a mindset of heaven----one of faith, provision, and overcoming (185).

I look at it this way, the birds can fly over your head, but they do not have to nest there. The thoughts are going to come, but you do not have to let them stay. We must trust God, rest in His Word, and bind and cast out those toxic thoughts. So the next time I got on my knees to pray and the devil tried to come at sis with that foolishness, I sent him packing!

Season 4: Saturating the Seed

During this season, you must pray, praise, worship, and confess God's Word. Prayer is an attitude. When we pray, there is a joining of forces with God. You should get into a place where all you do is put praise on everything. I know when times seem hard, praising him can be one of the hardest things to do. You can be bogged down with so much that you do not have a desire to pray. I have found myself experiencing this same feeling. However, we must remind ourselves regularly that no matter how bad it looks... PRAISE! I do not care how good it feels... PRAISE! Remember, it is not about you and your feelings; it is about God getting the glory out of your life and the situations you face. And for Him to do that, you must praise your way out. The Bible says that God inhabits the praises of His people, Psalm 22:3.

Once again, let us look at this through the eyes of a farmer. When a farmer plant seeds, their objective is to grow their crops to reap a harvest. Farmers must know what nutrients are needed. They are up early watering their crops, and they are faithful to the task. We must be the same way with the Word of God. It is time for us to have a mindset like a farmer. We need to search for God earnestly. Our soul should thirst for Him (Psalm 63:1-3).

Even though hardships may come, we must remember that they have come to make us stronger, they have come to test our faith, and most importantly, the difficulties have come to pass. God is still in it with you. He said He would never leave us, nor will He forsake us, and that is why we must understand the power of praise and worship. Believe it or not, it is your praise that has taken you this far, and it will be your praise that will bring you out and into your harvest. Do not let the rocks cry out in your place. Open your mouth and praise God. Hallelujah! **(Luke 19:40)**

Season 5: Removing the Weeds

This is one of the hardest seasons, if not challenging, for some of us. I know it was for me. To be honest, sometimes it still is. Weeding out the weeds is when we allow God to remove things or individuals from our lives that mean us no good. Note I stated, ***"allow God to remove,"*** this is where we tend to get in the way of God, and when that happens, we hinder our growth and block our blessings. I know this is something I did faithfully, and I try my best not to do it now.

Imagine you have a garden where you are planting the most beautiful flowers. One day you notice there are weeds in your flower bed. What do you do? Like any gardener, your first reaction is to pluck the weeds up to keep them from destroying the flowers.

Weeds are made to choke what is growing. They are ugly and very undesirable. If we look at our lives, we can see individuals or habits that are ugly and undesirable to God; those things or people are there only to choke what is in our hearts.

When I began to take my walk more seriously, God started removing people from my life. When the removal and separation of people started to happen, I was scared; these were people I knew for a long time, I considered them good friends. However, to God, it was time to weed out the weeds. I had to deal with the problems without all the distractions, so I could become what God wanted me to be in the future. The devil will use people for a season to make you miss your season. Let me say that again; the devil will use people for a season to make you miss your season.

I had to be extremely careful about what I "ate." I had to guard my heart because the enemy was angry, and he would test me just to find out what I knew. We must understand the process we are in; the enemy will try to keep you out of the will of God. As believers, we should always do a spiritual inventory and check our lives. Begin eliminating everything and everyone out of your life that goes against your faith and hinders your call. Weed out those undesirable weeds by renewing your mind and casting out those seeds by suffocating the enemy with the Word of God.

Some of us think we know what is best, so we try to rationalize why these habits or people should remain, but only the Lord knows what is best for us. He tells us in Jeremiah 29:11, *"For I know the plans I have for you,"* says the Lord. *"They are plans for good and not for disaster, to give you a future and a hope."* Just step aside and let God do what He does best.

Season 6: Season of Reaping

I do not know about you, but after going through those first five seasons, this is the one I have been waiting for...the season of harvest. The season of harvest is for those that continually cultivates their hearts, insert the seeds, fructify the ground, saturated the seeds, and removed the weeds. A farmer knows that there will be a reward at the end of his planting, especially if he has been taking care of the soil as he should. It is the same way with God when we do what is required. God promised us that we would have plentiful and live a life of abundance that we would not have room enough to receive. In this season, I could not be lazy, and I had to be steadfast and diligent. I could not listen to the ungodly or those that could not give a word of encouragement. What I mean by this is that when you are working in your season of harvest, those who do not understand it will speak negativity into your spirit and try to discourage you. I am sure you have heard someone say, "Why are you trying to go back to school at your age?"

When those kinds of questions come at you, I need for you to do three things; One, do not listen to those negative people; they want you to be as miserable as they are. Some folks do not want to see anyone grow and do well. Two, rebuke that devil right in his face. As soon as they speak against you with negativity, this means rebuke every Word with the Word of God, *"I can do all things through Christ"* (Philippians 4:13). And three, go hard and prove that devil wrong. Please understand, I am not calling the individual the devil. But let us be real; the enemy will use anybody to get you off track, including those closest to you, to make you lose focus. So, to sum this part up, do not fall for the devil's tricks.

Another reason why I love this season is because it lets us know that there is an expiration date on what we are facing. As I stated before, if you take hold of these seasons, begin to understand what season you are in, and apply them to your life, not only will they bless you, but you will have a greater understanding of how to bind the enemy. Remember, reaping is not only about your return. The most significant part to remember is that you still have work to do in your season of harvest. There was still a process I had to go through to reap the benefits and see the harvest manifestation. I had to believe and trust God with my whole heart. I had to be obedient, have a spirit of expectation, remain steadfast, and hold on to the provision of promise from God.

This is not the time to give up. You are close sis, you are right at the point of breakthrough bro...hang in there and reap the benefits of being obedient and from the suffering you endured. So, if we persevere just a little bit longer, push one more time, praise a little louder, and trust a bit more, we will reap if we faint not (Galatians 6:9).

"The nations will see your righteousness. World leaders will be blinded by your glory. And you will be given a new name by the Lord's own mouth."

Isaiah 62:2

Chapter Six

W hen I decided to live my life for the Father, I did not stop everything right away. Some can, but that did not occur with me. As I stated in the previous chapter, I knew I needed to make some severe changes, and it had to start with the people in my life. They were not good for me, and I was not good for them. I had to let them go; that was one of the hardest things I ever had to do. I did not stop smoking marijuana right away, but I still believed and trusted that the Lord would deliver me from that habit.

As I was going through my season of being delivered from smoking marijuana, the lust of women, and the married man, I begin to understand who I was. I also start to realize that I had to take my power back from the enemy.

The more I studied and meditated on God's Word, the more He revealed Himself to me. He was allowing me to see myself through His eyes...I am forgiven, I am loved, and that I am an overcomer. Not only did I have to see myself the way that God saw me, but I also had to change my belief system and my thoughts. I had to believe and think that I was all that God called me to be.

There was a time in my life where I was giving the enemy so

much authority over my mind, body, and soul that I lost myself. There were moments I would beat myself up whenever I gave in to temptation. The enemy knew my weak spots and what he thought could make me fall. He had me believing at times that I was not worthy of the Father's love because of the things I used to do. I did not know where I stopped, and the enemy began; that is how much control I gave to him.

I felt so unworthy to the point that I couldn't be used by God. Yet, he showed me the complete opposite. If you look at the people God used in the Bible, they all had issues; some were a little more extreme than others, but God still used them for His Glory. Abraham was a liar, and he even became the father of many nations. Noah was a drunk, but He used him to build the ark, and he found grace in our Lord's eyes. David was an adulterer who became the man after God's own heart. And let us not forget about Saul (who later became Paul), he persecuted Christians because they followed Jesus. Saul hated them, but one day a light shined from heaven, and Saul fell to the earth and heard a voice say to him, "Saul, Saul, why are you perse-cuting and oppressing me?" Saul asked who was speaking, and Jesus said it was He, the one Saul was persecuting (Acts 9:4). Even though Saul killed and imprisoned Christians, God still chose to use him for His glory.

So, as you can see, no matter what type of life you may have led in your past, God can change your life and use you for greatness. The only difference between these individuals and myself was that they were willing to be used and were obedient to what God instructed them to do. I, on the other hand, wanted to do everything my way. Let me help you and save you some time, let go and let God. Why keep trying it your way when obviously, it is not working. Whew! Release somebody today Holy Spirit!

Please, do not allow your past to dictate your future. There are so many men and women in the Bible that God used to reach His people. No longer do I allow my failures or my past to remain in my mind. I remind myself my past was just that...my past. I am still a useful tool for my Father's Kingdom, and so are you! (Philippians 1:6). Regardless of your mistakes and faults, you are not a failure. Yes, people will notice the fall but will not stick around long enough to witness the person getting back up after the fall. You need not bother yourself with that; remember that what the enemy used to destroy you failed because you are still here! Focus on His plan and purpose for you (Roman 8:28). You took the first step by getting back up.

"So, letting your sinful nature control your mind leads to death. But letting the Spirit control your mind leads to life and peace."

Romans 8:6

Chapter Seven

I t is so vital as a Believer to be spirit lead. The Bible says that the Holy Spirit will lead us into all truth, John 16:13. But for Him to do so, we must be submissive. When I realized I had a part to play in my deliverance, I began seeking things to help me with this process. I started being intentional about the things of God, such as reading my devotionals every day and working on renewing my mind. The bible states in Romans 12:2 *"don't copy the behavior and customs of this world, but let God transform you into a new person by changing the way you think. Then you will learn to know God's will for you, which is good and pleasing and perfect"*. God has given us one of the most incredible "how-to manuals," known to man, the Bible. It is totally up to us to pick it up and read the instructions. Sounds simple enough, huh? Well, it is simple; we are the ones who make it hard.

Some people cannot or will not take the initiative without being told. God would not take me by the hand and make me change. God has given us free will and if I wanted to change or know God's will for my life, then I had to stay in His Word. Well, let me hip you to something; Jesus Christ paid the ultimate price for you and me. He is not coming back to do it again. He has left instructions for us on how to live this Christian life. Trust me, I have learned that the hard way. I lost a lot before I could understand the process. You do not have to be hard-headed like me. You do not have to lose not one more thing to the enemy.

The enemy has an edge because many believers are still asleep while woke. God has many blessings for us, and until we get a hold of this life called salvation, we will never experience the Kingdom here on earth. All that Jesus went through, the suffering, beating, spit on, and mocked, was for our benefit. Jesus sacrificed His life, so we can have a right to the tree of life and live a blessed and fruitful life full of abundance (Revelations 22:14 & John 10:10). My question to you is, do you want that abundant life here on earth, or would you prefer to wait until you get to heaven? How would you feel when you get there, and God shows you all the blessings He had stored up for you, even the ones you didn't pray for?

I had to make a choice; either I want to live in sin or walk-in righteousness, and I needed the Holy Spirit to help me make this choice. To do this and keep myself focused on God; I began to surround myself with positive people, prayer warriors, and those who had an encouraging word for me.

The first thing I do is fast. When we fast, we desire to hear from the Lord. Fasting doesn't do anything for the God; the benefits are for you. The reward is for us to be closer to Him and to hear from Him. Because I wanted fasting to be a lifestyle for me, I had to be consistent, committed, and discipline myself to do it more. To move toward this, I decided to set aside three days every month to fast and pray (seek God on fasting for yourself) because this was essential to my spiritual growth. I was at a crossroad where I felt it was time to do whatever necessary to make changes in my life. I had to do whatever I needed to do to put my flesh into submission. Remember, my objective through this process was to live a life that was spirit lead.

As I was going through my deliverance season, there were certain scriptures that I meditate on for encouragement. For instance, one was about seven more demons that will return far worse than the ones before. *"When a defiling evil spirit is expelled from someone, it drifts along through the desert looking for an oasis, some unsuspecting soul it can bedevil. When it doesn't find anyone, it says, 'I'll go back to my old haunt.' On return it finds the person spotlessly clean, but vacant. It then runs out and rounds up seven other spirits more evil than itself and they all move in, whooping it up. That person ends up far worse off than if he'd never gotten cleaned up in the first place. That's what this generation is like: You may think you have cleaned out the junk from your lives and gotten ready for God, but you weren't hospitable to my kingdom message, and now all the devils are moving back in"* (Matthew 12:43-45). Man, if this scripture did not make me walk straight and reading it from the Message Bible hit differently.

Once you turn away from those habits, do not look back even when the enemy tries to use familiar things; pray for strength and keep moving. Most importantly, ask God into your life by receiving His son Jesus into your heart and then seek Him to infill you with the power of the Holy Spirit. Accepting the Holy Spirit in our lives is what fills the house, and therefore demons can no longer dwell there.

When I wanted to break any strongholds in my life, I had to put myself on a 21-day challenge. After 21 days of doing something, it becomes a habit. This was a huge test for me, and to be honest, it was one of the hardest challenges I ever faced. I did not want to give up my friends, but at the same time, I was tired of doing the same things over and over. I meditated on the word of God. day and night because only then will you prosper and succeed in all you do (Joshua 1:8). Also, Psalms 1:2 states, *"But they delight in the law of the Lord, meditating on it day and night."*

As you can see, meditation is essential. Therefore, stay in His Word so you will have evidence to show those who do not believe that God is real. When I used to tell my friends that I was going to stop smoking, they would always laugh. They were not laughing because they thought I was joking; they laughed because I was still doing what they were, which caused them not to believe me. When people do not believe in you, it can be hard for them to see your vision. Better yet, it's even harder for them to understand it. However, your vision isn't for them to understand, it's for you!

In Matthew 13:11 and 13, the disciples asked Jesus why He speaks to the people in parables. Jesus responded by saying that the disciples are permitted to understand the Kingdom of Heaven's secrets, but others are not.

"I have hidden your word in my heart, that I might not sin against you."

Psalm 119:11

Chapter Eight

I f there is no growth in you, then you can easily be cut down. Once I received the Word, I had to guard my heart and the Word. As I stated earlier, the enemy was coming to kill the Word that I received. The enemy was also coming to steal the peace and revelation that I received and destroy the power that I gained from that very same Word.

The enemy was throwing things at me to get me off course, but what he did not know was that he was working for me. Oh yeah, the enemy is always working for you. He is just too stupid to realize it (Romans 8:28). I began to accept and welcome everything that came my way, whether it was good or bad. It increased my faith and trust in the Father, and that is all that mattered. No matter what the enemy was throwing at me, I was not going to break. He was using and will continue to use the enemy to get us in a place where He wants us to be. If we get a few bruises along the way, then so be it; God will heal us in the process. Those scars will speak of dedication, patience, faith, and warrior who endured as a good soldier. I was tested in the fire and came out as pure gold.

I went through preparing my heart, planting the seed, and fertilizing the ground; now, I had to begin watering that seed. To do this, I had to read the Word more, pray without ceasing, praise Him daily, and worship Him always.

Prayer is the most important because it is a joining of forces with the Father. In prayer is when you can hear from the Father, receive guidance, and renew your strength.

As I previously stated; because of my sins, there were times I would allow the enemy to put negative thoughts in my head; he would have me to believe that the Father was not listening to me. The enemy had me feeling as if I was not worthy of the Father's love. "Why are you praying? After what you did, how can you believe that He hears you? There's no need to pray." These are the thoughts that the enemy would use to keep me in bondage.

He wanted me to believe that I was worthless and undeserving of the Father's love. And because I was allowing him to have full reign over my mind, his tactics were working; until I made up in my mind that my season with the enemy was over. Oh yes, he has a season too, but it is up to you how long that season with him will last.

When I read that my first thought was "this sounds like being in bondage. If you do not want to be in bondage and never seeing or experiencing deliverance, then learn to break free of the enemy's hold of your mind. As I stated before, when the enemy controls your mind, he has control of you, which is where things can become very dangerous. I read a devotional by Tony Evans called "Who Controls Your Thoughts?" Evans stated that "one reason satan's strongholds are so powerful is that they become entrenched and he can get you to buy into a lie that your situation is hopeless". Evans goes on to say that "once you give in to and adopt this line of thinking, these fortresses become difficult to remove. Your behavior deteriorates even more since all of us act according to who we believe we are".

When I reflect on my life, I can see that I was heading in that direction. I was getting to a point where I was on my way to allowing the enemy to have full control over my life. I had to repent, ask for forgiveness, and learn that prayer is one of the keys that I can use for any situation.

In Dr. Cindy Trimm's book, The Rules of Engagement {the art of strategic prayer and spiritual warfare}, she reassures us by saying that "prayer is the key to effective spiritual warfare. And that prayer releases God's flow into your life so that you can defeat the enemy." When we are weak during our various battles, prayer is the link that will keep us connected to God's strength.

Both Jesus and Paul emphasized prayer's importance, noting that people always pray and never give up (Luke 18:1, 1 Timothy 2:1). Prayer includes asking and getting answers from the Father. Note, it says that **"prayer includes asking,"** which means asking is only a part of the solution. There is also confession, adoration, thanksgiving, and fellowship.

Prayers of confession are when you "confess" your wrongdoing to God, or it can be the thoughts you have towards others. It can also be hurt or envy you may hold in your heart. Confess those sins to the Lord, and He will keep His Word by being faithful and just to forgive us for those sins (1 John 1:9).

If we can live our lives without confessing our sins, we contradict His Word. We make Him out to be false and a liar. And there is no way His Word is in us. During this time of my life, I strongly desired to experience deliverance from all I was going through. For this to happen, I had to activate my prayer life and be consistent. You must develop a prayer life because not praying is considered a sin (1 Samuel 12:23).

The last step with prayer is how we fellowship with the Father. By nature, prayer is talking with the Father. It is the basis of a victorious Christian life. When someone fellowship with another person, they communicate regularly or hang out to get to know one another. This is the same way we should be with God. He wants us to be in fellowship with Him regularly. Fellowship is having a close relationship with God. We can share our thoughts and have a spirit of obedience to Him through His Son, Jesus Christ. If we say that we are in fellowship with God but still live our lives in darkness, we speak falsely, which means we do not live and practice the truth (1 John 1:6). Therefore, you need to be or stay in fellowship with God (1 John 1:3).

God created us in His own image. Being in harmony with God is not for Him to get to know us but for us to get to know Him. We tell God that he is our everything. We tell him how much we adore Him. And yet, we lack in our communication with him. When you love someone, you want to make them happy. You want to show them you care by your actions. As parents, we have that feeling towards our children. It is the same way with God. Our love for God should be like the love we have for our children multiplied by a billion.

Throughout my walk with God, I have come to understand how extraordinary being in fellowship with God can be. The more time I spend with Him, the more I get to know Him, and He gets to know me. Remember, the closer you draw to God, the closer He draws to you. However, you must understand that no matter what you are facing, God is worthy of praise!

"Confess your sins to each other and pray for each other so that you may be healed. The earnest prayer of a righteous person has great power and produces wonderful results."

James 5:16

Chapter Nine

P rayer, along with action is vital in our Christian walk, so much so that I wanted to spend a little time on it. To have an effective prayer life, I had to change how I prayed, and most importantly, I had to BELIEVE in what I was asking of Him.

Also, when you pray, always have a humble heart. Praying with a humble heart is the most effective way to hear from God. A heart that is humbled is a heart that can be penetrated with God's Word. Jesus pointed out that the Father listened to a humble person's prayer rather than that of a proud Pharisee. *"I tell you; this man went down to his home justified (forgiven and made upright and in right standing with God), rather than the other man; for everyone who exalts himself will be humbled, but he who humbles himself will be exalted."* (*Luke 18:14 AMP*)

Below is a model I use to build my prayer life/spirit man.

We Must Obey Him: *Time*

As the bible states, obedience is better than sacrifice. If God gives you a specific time that He wants you to spend with Him and choose to do other things, you are operating in disobedience and will often miss the blessings of God. I know that life happens, sometimes we fall short of doing what is required of us, believe me, I am guilty of this myself. However, we must make a conscious decision to do what God has told us to do. There indeed should be a point where we begin to obey what God says. If He tells us not to do something and we, do it anyway, we are operating in sin. But when we follow God, we are in His will and can stretch out our hands and receive what we ask. We are doing what He said, and we are doing what pleases Him (1 John 3:22).

We Must Confess our Sins: *Release*

Confession is when we have done something wrong and admit to it. However, when I pray, I often say, "Father forgive me of my sins, the ones I know about, and the ones I don't know about." I mean, think about it, we could have looked at someone funny or had a thought about a person, not ever considering our actions to be sinful. Confession is so important when it comes to God, the omniscient one. He knows everything anyway, which means you cannot hide anything from Him. Not acknowledging our sins is another way to block our blessings (1 John 1:9 AMP). We serve a God that knows our thoughts before we even think them, so you might as well confess your sins, repent, and move on.

We Must Abide in Jesus: *Stand*

To abide with Christ means to conform, to act in accordance to, and to stand. God's Word is life, which means it gives life to all those dead situations. We are faced with problems that may try to over-whelm you; that is your time to conform to the ways of God. It is during that time that you must act according to God's Word. You cannot say that you believe God if when your back is up against the wall, you crumble like a piece of paper. No matter what you are facing, if you remain under Jesus, linked to Him in all areas of your life, then there is nothing too big or too small that you cannot ask of Him (John 15:7 AMP). There is absolutely nothing that can form against you that God the Father will allow to prosper. Abide in Him, and He shall abide in you! When you have done all that you could... just stand on His promises.

Danielle Johnson

We Must ask According to the Will of the Father: *Your will be His Will*

What we do or say should be done in the will of God. Individuals have struggled in this area because they may not understand the purpose of being in His will, which is ok. He will reveal it to you soon enough. While you are in the will of God, there is a sense of boldness that comes over you. You are more confident and determine to do what God has commanded. The best way to find out God's Will for your life is to read His Word (1 John 5:14).

We Must ask in Faith: *Embrace*

This is so important! If you do not believe in what you are speaking into the atmosphere or praying for, you are only wasting your time. This Christian walk is a walk of FAITH; either you will believe it or not. I hate to burst your bubble, but there are no in-between, no gray areas in this walk. It is about trusting GOD and His Word even though the world and the fleshly system want you to go through life picking and choosing what you want to believe, whereas, with God, there is no cherry-picking.

Be bold, have faith, confidence, and be very specific when you approach the throne of God. Know that He is a God of detail who never falters on His promises. Ask and believe and watch God do it. Believe what you are saying and leave it at that. *That's why I urge you to pray for absolutely everything, ranging from small to large. Include everything as you embrace this God-life, and you'll get God's everything.* (Mark 11:24 Message Bible)

We Must Have Pure Motives When We Pray: *Sincere*

God knows what we need, and He knows what we will do with everything that He gives to us. He knows if you will be a blessing to others or if you are going to be selfish and think of only yourself. Let me ask you this, have you ever asked for something with an intent behind it? For example, you ask God to bless you with transportation; however, your reason for wanting a car it's not only because you need one, but you also feel that since everyone doesn't want to give you a ride; then you'll be the same way when you get a car. So, you pray

56

with ill intent, which is not of God. This is what God calls praying amiss. **James 4:13** informs us that when we ask for what we should not have because we want it for our pleasure, we only want it to satisfy our flesh.

Our prayers should always be faith-based, specific, but most importantly, wholesome. Remember, we have the authority to access the Kingdom. However, we must access it with a pure heart. Our intent should be to bring glory to God's name.

"Therefore, come out from among unbelievers, and separate yourselves from them, says Lord. Don't touch their filthy things, and I will welcome you."

2 Corinthians 6:17

Chapter Ten

Now that we have a better understanding of prayer, let us get back to the seasons. I had to begin removing things and people that were hindering my spiritual walk. This was the most challenging task because I had to let some of my close friends go. I will not lie; I remember feeling nervous and scared because I was so used to having them around, not seeing them seemed to be hard and scary.

In Psalms 1:1, it says, *"Blessed is the man that walks not in the counsel of the ungodly, nor stands in the way of sinners, nor sit in the seat of the scornful."* So, this is who I had to be, who I desired to become, who God created me to be, and that is a "happy or blessed" woman.

The first step to becoming this person was to change my environment. Sometimes we can be so comfortable with the way our lives are going that we begin to lose who we are. Have you ever been around people for a period, and eventually, you started acting like them? Your speech changed, your behavior changed, and sadly your way of thinking changed. That is called "conforming to the things of this world." (Romans 12:2)

Everyone in my circle was doing the same things; smoking, drinking, partying, and unemployed; we were some broke, high people who were letting life pass us by. I finally got tired of being sick and tired. Thus, I decided to transform my life.

As I stated before, the steps I took to make this transformation were simple, but it was challenging. However, I made up my mind to change, and this was the most crucial step. Not only did I have a mind to change, but I also had the heart to change. I surrounded myself with individuals who were going in the positive direction I wanted to go.

My conversations were with individuals who uplifted me, prayed with me and for me. Most importantly, I never gave up on God. No matter how frustrating it became, no matter how many times I may have fallen short, which was a lot of times--I continue to stand because I believe in God.

You cannot walk this walk of salvation with individuals who do not understand where you are going in your life or see your vision. Once I understood that letting people go or removing myself away from them was to my benefit, it was not hard for me at all. Holding on to those people and those habits was only making this walk harder than it was. The Father never said it was going to be easy, and trust me, it is not. However, you have an advocate right there with you every step of the way. He never left my side, even when I was deeply in my mess. He was right there, all along, waiting patiently, for me to come back to His loving arms. And no matter how much I messed up, He never stopped loving me, and for that, I am so grateful.

"He is the Holy Spirit, who leads into all truth. The world cannot receive him, because it isn't looking for him and doesn't recognize him. But you know him, because he lives with you now and later will be in you."

John 14:17

Chapter Eleven

As I matured in Christ, I began to learn just how important a role the Holy Spirit plays in our day-to-day life. When the Holy Spirit dwells on the inside, Grace and Mercy shall follow you. Without the Holy Spirit, it is hard to live in this life. The Holy Spirit should control every aspect of your life. The Spirit leads and guides you into all truth. He is a comforter and road map to where God wants to take you. He is the one that helped me through those rough times in my life. It is only through the Holy Spirit that we can look through the lens of scripture for us to understand the things of God.

When I was working through old habits, the Holy Spirit gave me scriptures to meditate on. When my flesh started to rise and call out for a man's touch, it was the Holy Spirit that gave me strength not to give in to temptation. He always provided a way of escape.

Jesus said that He would leave us a comforter that will bring us that unspeakable joy, the kind that surpasses all understanding. But this is not where it stops; the Holy Spirit is our guide, peace, and happiness. He is the one that we can depend on. In John 16:13, John expounded on this by saying, *"When the Spirit of truth comes, he will guide you into all truth. He will not speak on his own but will tell you what he has heard. He will tell you about the future."*

I want all of us, to be in a place in our walk with God-that we lean on the Holy Spirit for everything. And I do mean everything, no matter how big or small the issue may seem to us; the Holy Spirit wants us to include Him in it.

Dr. William Evans, the author of The Great Doctrine of the Bible, says, "Many can testify to the blessing that came into their lives when they came to know the Holy Spirit, not merely as a gracious influence but as an ever-present, loving friend and helper." He goes on to say that "through Sonship and membership in the Kingdom of God come only through the regenerating of The Holy Spirit. It is the Spirit that quickeneth. Just as Jesus was begotten of the Holy Spirit, so must every child of God who is to be an heir of the Kingdom." (pgs 57 & 61)

When we live our lives through the Spirit, it will help us live our lives authentically, our true selves. Dr. Cindy Trimm wrote a book titled, *The 40 Day Soul Fast Your Journey to Authentic Living*—in this book, she gives an outline or narrative outlook on how to live your true self. Your authentic self! In the book, she asked a question that stuck out to me and made me reevaluate my life. She asked, "what is it that keeps you from being your best self and living your best life filled with joy, peace, and happiness?"

Is not this what we want; to live a life filled with peace? But to experience this way of living, we must put in the effort to do so. However, when people do not have a positive mindset and allow strongholds to overtake them, they will never walk with certainty nor run with purpose.

Our thoughts can either hinder us or call us into action and eventually bless us. I heard someone say, "If you think on something long enough, you will give birth to reality." All of us are one decision away from having our destiny fulfilled or our future destroyed. I believe in this wholeheartedly. When I decided to give my life to Christ, I didn't know what to expect; the only thing I knew was that the decision I made would impact my life and those around me.

Even though it's been an uphill battle, I never regretted the choice I made to be honest with you and sharing my story; if it weren't for the Holy Spirit leading and guiding me, I wouldn't have made it through. The Holy Spirit is the reason why I stand; it was through the Holy Spirit that I was able to let go of those ungodly habits, and it is through the Holy Spirit that I continue to fight!

To have a relationship with the Father through the Holy Spirit is something I never take lightly. I aim to be mindful of the power that I carry within me. When you have the Holy Spirit residing in you, there is nothing that can stop you. We serve a God that has the entire world in His hand. The entire WORLD! That means that we should not have to want or worry about anything. I am continually reminding myself of that whenever those thoughts of self-doubt try to rise.

As believers, we must understand that this battle we are fighting is a spiritual one and the only way to destroy a spirit is by the Spirit. God's Word is a primary weapon given to believers. We must use the Word daily, not just when dealing with trouble, but every day. I want you to know and understand that I am also saying to myself what I am saying to you. As I stated before, work to remove all those carnal thoughts as they come out of your mind and become spiritually minded.

"Charm is deceptive, and beauty does not last; but a woman who fears the Lord will greatly praised."

Proverbs 31:30

Chapter Twelve

I am so excited to have reached this chapter. This last chapter is dedicated to all of us who felt like we were not good enough for anyone, those of us who thought that we were only good for sexual pleasure and nothing more.

When I was a teen, I never understood how important it was to wait for the one. I think it took my son's birth and my relationship with God the Father for me to understand the significance of knowing my worth.

I know there are times where you may have had someone close to you speak negative words into your Spirit. Such as "you'll never be anything," but He said that you could do all things through Christ (Philippians 4:13). They said, "you are worthless," but He said you are more valuable than rubies (Proverbs 31). The moment you start seeing yourself through the eyes of the Lord will be the day that you take back your peace, joy, and power from the enemy. That is what I had to do, take back my power. Whew!

It is ok to have issues or go through trials and tribulations. They only come to make you stronger. Having or dealing with issues is not the problem. The problem is allowing the issues to have you.

As I stated in a previous chapter, I used to use my body as a tool to get the love I was so desperately seeking. However, the guy would use an imitation of what love was to get my body, and just like that, I would give it away. I am learning every day how to value myself and just how precious a gift I have to offer to my future husband. Individuals have told me that being single is the best time of your life, especially if you are a believer.

Well, I beg to differ on this topic; I believe it is rough to be a single Christian woman. Trying to get through this waiting stage can be so paralyzing that you want to rush God or step in the way of His timing and try to do things your way. You begin to think about areas in your life that need fixing, then you start seeking God and asking what have you done or what more can you do to receive who He has for you. BIG MISTAKE!

Even though I want to be married, that does not mean that something is missing or that I do not feel whole without someone. I came to a point in my life where I did not want to continue giving away a gift that God said I should only share with my husband. Paul reaffirmed this when he wrote a letter to the Roman church, *"And so, dear brothers and sisters, I plead with you to give your bodies to God because of all he has done for you. Let them be a living and holy sacrifice—the kind he will find acceptable. This is truly the way to worship him"* (Romans 12:1).

There was a point in my life when I didn't feel complete, I felt a void so strong in my life, and a hole so deep in my heart that I thought there was nothing to fill it. I felt so incomplete...not whole. Now, if you feel that you are not complete or whole until that one comes into your life, then you will never be complete. In James 1:4, *"So let it grow, for when your endurance is fully developed, you will be perfect and complete, needing nothing"* (New Living Translation). All that changed the day I decided to give my life to Christ. I finally felt whole, that emptiness was filled.

At times, I feel like I am caught between a rock and a hard place. God says not to fornicate, (1 Corinthians 6:18) and on top of that, I have heard people say that God said that masturbation is a BIG no, this is because of the un-pure thoughts that come with the act. I am still out on this one...I need to see some scriptures. I am just keeping it real.

When I decided to become celibate, my first thought was "oh this is going to be easy." I was under the impression that since I was single, I did not have a thing to worry about...how wrong I was! I cannot speak for everyone that has gone through this stage in their life, but for me, it truly has been a challenge to live a celibate life. Please do not take this the wrong way; I enjoy my alone times. However, it is challenging because I am trying to remain abstinent until marriage. Whew child, sis is struggling. Flesh on fire and every-thing lol. But I am hanging in there. Now do not get me wrong, I know marriage is not all about sex, but my goodness, a human touch every now and then would be great.

It gets lonely at times, especially during those rainy nights. Come on ladies, you know what I am talking about. It is a battle, but in the end, it will all be worth it.

I know that my faithfulness to God will open the door for me to receive who He has set aside just for me. I must lean on the Lord daily and call on the Holy Spirit and fire for strength. With that being said, consume yourself with the things of God. Chase after Him and let Him bring those desires to pass in His timing, so you can be whole and standing complete in Him. Until you become one with God, you will never be able to become one with anybody else. God should be the only one that you seek after to make you complete or whole.

It's alright to love yourself, date yourself, and embrace your season of singleness. I am now in a place where I can proudly say that I am the prize which in turn means that I know my worth. I don't know why I haven't met him yet and I can't begin to understand it, all I know is that I must continue to trust God in this process and allow the Holy Spirit to lead and guide me.

As I close this book, I would like to leave you with some words of encouragement and a prayer for guidance, peace, and strength. Also, I want you to make this prayer personal, remember this is about you and your salvation.

WORDS OF ENCOURAGEMENT

First, I want you to know that God loves you, and there is nothing you could do or say that can make Him love you any less. His desire is for ALL His children to come to the knowledge of Christ. He does not want to see any of us in pain, sick, lack, or worry. God said that everything belongs to Him. If He can take care of the birds in the sky that do not do anything for Him, don't you think He can do so much more for you. God says in **Matthew 6:26-27** *"look at the birds of the air; they do not sow or reap or store away in barns, and yet your heavenly Father feeds them. Are you not much more valuable than they? Can anyone of you by worrying add a single hour to your life?"*

We live in a world where we want things to come to us without any work being done, but that's not reality, especially not with God. There's work that we must do if we want blessings from God. He said in **Matthew 6:33**, *"But seek ye first the kingdom of God, and His righteousness; and all these things shall be added unto you."* This means that everything you desire will be added to your life when you begin to seek God first and not after you have sought after everyone else.

Nobody said it was going to be easy. I know life gets hard, but you must remember that God is in this with you. He only wants what is best for you. *"For I know the plans I have for you,"* declares the Lord, *"plans to prosper you and not to harm you, plans to give you hope and a future"* (**Jeremiah 29:11**). Continue to keep a praise on your lips, seek God first, stay in His will, do not give up, and watch how God begins to move in your life.

PRAYER

Father, today I ask for Your forgiveness in the name of Jesus. You said if I confess my sins, You will be faithful and just, to forgive me of those sins. I ask that You forgive me for sins of omission, things I should have done and did not do and sins of commission things I should not have done but did.

Lord, You are my everything. You are all I need in my life. I give all glory and honor to Your name. You have provided for my family and me, You have been faithful to me like no one has ever been. I thank You for being my comforter, my peace, and my joy.

Father God, I know Your Word is life, and it will bring me out of any hardships I face. Lord, your Word says that You will never leave me nor forsake me and as I look over my life, I can see how You have not abandoned me. Your Word is true. I thank You for progress, for healing and deliverance. Thank You for loving me. God, this year is moving quickly, I am looking forward to what You have in store for me.

The road ahead will not be easy at times, but with You before me who can be against me. Holy Spirit, I ask that You lead and guide me into all truth. Lord, I ask that You renew my strength because all the strength I had on yesterday is long gone. I am facing many trials, but I know that You are working things out for me and this includes the good and bad. Your Word says that all things are working together for my good and I am standing on that. Lord, I asked that You would cover me with favor as I continue to walk in faith.

In Jesus Name, I pray.

"Who can find a virtuous woman and capable woman? She is more precious than rubies."

Proverbs 31:10

She Knows Her Worth Poem

As a little girl, she sometimes felt alone.
Her father died, and her mother tried her best.
even though she was faced with a lot, she mastered every test.
The day she tried God was the day her new life was birthed,
because then and only then did she begin to understand her worth.
As she rises early every morning, there is a power that she displays.
she is a woman who became to know her worth. The love she has for
herself does not compare to the love; Christ has shown her each day.
She does not need a man to show her how valuable she is, God tells
her daily in His Word because she is one of His. She sees herself in
Proverbs 31:10, a virtuous woman. because she finally knows her
worth.

Danielle Johnson

Supporting Scriptures

Armor (Ephesians 6:12-17)

Battle (2 Chronicles 20:15-17)

Cleansing (Psalm 51:1-11)

Delight (Psalms 37:4-5)

Fasting (Mark 9:29)

Faith (Hebrews 11:6)

Fornication (1 Corinthians 6:18)

Fruits of the Spirit (Galatians 5:22-23)

Holy Spirit (John 16:13)

Hope & Future (Jeremiah 29:11)

Jehovah-Jireh (Philippians 4:19)

Joy (Nehemiah 8:10)

Peace (Isaiah 26:3)

Praise (Psalms 150)

Pray (2 Chronicles 7:14)

Re-dedicating your Life (1 John 1:9)

Salvation (Romans 10:8-10)

Seeking God (Matthew 6:33)

Strength (Isaiah 40:31)

Temptation (1 Corinthians 10:13)

Thanksgiving (Psalms 100:4-5)

Trust (Proverbs 3:5-6)

Victory (Deuteronomy 20:4)

Virtuous woman (Proverbs 31:10-31)

Wait (Psalms 27:14)

Worry (Matthew 6:25-32)

Yoke (Matthew 11:28-30)

Bibliography

Evans, T. (2022) *Who Controls your Thoughts.*

Evans, W. (1992) *The Great Doctrine of the Bible.* Moody Publishers

Trimm, C. (2008) The Rules of Engagement {the art of strategic prayer and spiritual warfare}. Charisma House 140

Trimm, C. (2014) *Commanding your Morning Daily Devotional.* Charisma House 185

About the Author

Danielle Johnson is a mom. Her favorite scripture is Jeremiah 29:11. She graduated from Tidewater Community College in 2013 with her Associates of Applied Science Degree in Management. She graduated in May 2023 from Regent University with her Bachelor's Degree in Professional Studies with a concentration in Teacher Education.

She has written two children's books titled Chubb the Chipmunk and Ashley Nalayla goes to the Nail Salon. She is a featured author in an anthology titled Love Hope Faith. As an author, her goal is to minister to as many readers as possible through her writing. Her desire is for readers to feel the authenticity of her story while making a difference in their lives. She hopes that the words she shares on each page reaches their hearts and are not looked at as mere words on paper, but that they feel her heart beat through her words.

Danielle's desire is for her readers to be able to see themselves in the text, and prayerfully through the Holy Spirit, be delivered and set free. Her mission to accomplish her desires with reaching her readers is through being transparent, realistic and relatable. She wants to use her testimony as a platform to minister and help women who are broken in their spirit.

For I know the plans I have for you," says the Lord. "They are plans for good and not for disaster, to give you a future and a hope. Jeremiah 29:11